STUDIES IN MODERN EUROPEAN LITERATURE AND THOUGHT

General Editor
ERICH HELLER
Professor of German
in the University College of Swansea

FRANÇOIS MAURIAC

FRANÇOIS MAURIAC

BY

MARTIN JARRETT-KERR, C.R.

NEW HAVEN
YALE UNIVERSITY PRESS
1954

Printed in the United States of America

For

WLADIMIR WEIDLÉ

CONTENTS

122607

PREFACE

A short study such as the following must be selective. Writing for an English audience I have been governed to some extent by two assumptions: that my readers will be largely ignorant of those works of M. Mauriac that have appeared so far only in French, but that they will have ready access to the novels that have been translated into English. If I have sometimes given the former more attention than is their due, it is to fill in an otherwise incomplete picture.

I have used where available to me the excellent translations of the novels by Mr Gerard Hopkins. Their merit is patent to all. Thanks are due to Messrs Eyre & Spottiswoode for permission to quote them.

Two debts of gratitude in particular I must pay: to Dr T. V. Benn, of the French Department in the University of Leeds, for information about and the loan of books, and Mr Graham Clarke, of the Anglo-French Literary Services Ltd, London, for constant help and advice.

I

Background

Newman believed that if the fields and the sky give us the impression they do of purity and innocence, it is because nature was created before man the sinner, and took no part in Adam's crime. But from the time that man first lives on the earth, lies down to sleep or to cry, to the time he sinks and returns to dust, nature has become human. She is made of the ash of man's sin and has no resemblance to what she was when she was born in the thought of God . . . We cannot imagine the world as it was before man appeared . . . I doubt whether desert islands and uninhabited lands sing the glory of God as clearly as our old countryside proclaims the struggles and the sufferings of man.[1]

Biography is never literary criticism; and in the case of François Mauriac it could never even attempt to be. What does one need to know, apart from his works, about the uneventful life of this novelist, critic, editor and (dare we say?) tyrant of letters? Born in 1885; made a member of the Académie française in 1933; a denouncer of the Franco régime in the Spanish war; on the side of the Resistance during the occupation—he even wrote a *Cahier Noir* for the secret periodical *Éditions de Minuit*, and in 1943 some signed articles of his appeared in the Swiss, Portugese and Balkans press, of which one was quoted by Général de Gaulle in a radio talk to the French before the liberation; but he refused to take part in the purges after the war;[2] now a powerful influence in the direction of the literary organs *Figaro*, *Figaro Littéraire*, and *La Table Ronde*. Here are the bare bones—and they tell us little. What is far more important, to prepare us for and even to explain the strength and the limitations of his work, is the picture of his home and childhood. No subtleties of Freudian analysis are required to show us the permanent influence upon him of the Landes (the marsh-and-pine country round Bordeaux) and the people it breeds. A people with small minds, tight fists and deep roots; with a loyalty difficult to distinguish from tenaciousness. And their roots go so deep into the soil that they are entangled with all the other roots that snuggle there: hence the frequent identi-

1 *Journal* (1932-39), p. 32.
2 North, pp. 64-5.

9

fication of man with his crops. Sometimes, indeed, man even takes on the less important role of the two: 'Why was it that the heath villages never caught fire?', mused Thérèse Desqueyroux, during a time of scorching weather. 'It seemed to her unjust that it should always be the trees that the flames chose, never the human beings.'[1]

The worst horror is that with the coming of the storm will come the hail, and smash the vine-harvest:

> The Bishop had ordered public prayers for rain: personally I'd rather have drawn up a pact with the drought. With us the ground is firm enough for the vines to be able to do without water for months; they stand up like strapping fellows right in the furnace and in the midst of sweltering summers they sing the Song of the Three Children ... For it's a miracle if rain comes without a storm, and the storm brings hail ... In the thickets of the sky these snarling beasts come rushing out in packs, like wolves: they invade us on all sides. If you hope to escape the one that comes from the west, you won't get away without the one that lies in ambush behind the hornbeam trees in the south, the monster with its lowering forehead. Sometimes it hesitates, seems to draw away—as happened last September 8th; and then suddenly it changed its mind: a furious icy wind hurled the hail-storm against us. In the tumult we thought we heard the trees crying in terror.[2]

Small wonder that the union of man and harvest in a wedding of empathy should give birth to an obstinate, sturdy peasantry and a close, cautious bourgeoisie:

> A prudent, circumspect, canny race, whose insurance policies are paid up for time and eternity.[3]

'And eternity'; for here eternity is still assumed, however casually, and before the midnight mass at Christmas the servants watched over the masters' reserved seats up till 11 o'clock at night.[4] Nor is it purely formal. There are occasional outbursts even of a demonic sort of paganism which testify to a stormy past history. Félicité Cazenave, for instance,

---

1 *Thérèse*, p. 70.
2 *Journal*, p. 36.
3 *Commencements*, p. 102.
4 Ibid., p. 102.

believed in nothing that she could not touch. She had been born in the days when only a few sandy tracks linked the Landes with the outside world. The 'Terror' had driven the priests away. Her own mother had not made her First Communion till the day she was married. At the beginning of the previous century the children of the Landes had had but one religion, that of the implacable and fiery sun; had known but one Almighty, the blaze that burned the pines—a swift-moving, unapproachable God who left in the wake of his progress a host of smoking torches.[1]

While on the other hand, from the midst of the pious mechanical murmur of self-protective devotion, there arises from time to time a genuine anguished cry of beseeching. Mauriac remembers his grandfather's last visit from Langon, the day before his death—Mauriac himself was five at the time.

He sat down heavily in an armchair and looked at the photographs of the deceased, among whom were some of his own relations. 'What a cemetery!' he sighed. The next day he went to revisit all the places he loved, his property at Malagar, the alms-house he administered; then after dinner he went round to some old friends where he used to make up a hand at 'boston' every evening. And it was here that the supernatural intervened. 'M. Mauriac', asked the old lady, one of the two friends, 'I'm going to Benediction; will you come with me?' My grandfather had been a strong anti-clerical all his life, and a declared enemy of the Marist fathers of Verdelais. Though he had softened (under the influence of my mother, of whom he was very fond) he hadn't set a foot inside Church for years. To the surprise of everyone, he agreed to go with the old lady, and appeared to be very recollected right till the end of Adoration. On the way back, in the road, in front of the Misses Merlet, he stumbled, and collapsed. They carried him as far as his bed. He had time to reply to a friend who was begging him to pray: 'It is faith that saves us', and he joined his hands.[2]

It is worth remembering this authentic incident, coming as it did at the boy's most impressionable age, when we come to consider the 'death-bed conversions' in Mauriac's novels.

[1] *Genetrix*, p.155f.
[2] *Commencements*, p. 12f.

Indeed, I have not seen it pointed out that these very words, 'la foi nous sauve', are put into the mouth of Numa Cazenave, the husband of old Félicité Cazenave, who died while his wife was away with their son, Fernand. In fact, the whole scene of Cazenave's death is taken almost verbatim from Mauriac's account of his childhood.[1]

So many critics have objected to these conversions on the threshold of death—of Gabriel Gradère,[2] of Louis, the rapacious, jealous grandfather,[3] of Irène de Blénauge,[4] of Fabien Dézaymeries (though here it is a mortal sickness from which in fact he recovers),[5] as well as that of old Numa Cazenave just mentioned. They have contended that such conversions are false, artificial and unconvincing. So it is only fair to remember the closeness of their resemblance to actual historical instances of the same kind of thing. Of course, the critics may go on to say that even such genuine instances may lack conviction within the novel, because of some failure of presentation or technique, and that it is with the novels that they as critics are concerned. Sometimes this is true, as we shall see in our third chapter. But one suspects that this is not always the real objection, that this judgement by these critics would be passed equally severely on the cases in real life, and that behind the judgement there lies an irritable (and understandable) resistance to the whole reign of what might be called 'conversion melodrama' in early twentieth-century literary France.

That it was a reign, we cannot doubt. Journals and correspondence are as much under its domination as novels, and the Claudel-Gide letters have been a sort of *atelier* in which lesser artists have been unfortunately trained. One of the striking flaws in what is otherwise among the most impressive of Mauriac's novels, *The Knot of Vipers*, occurs when Louis suddenly notes in his diary-cum-confession-cum-autobiography:

After my death, among my papers you [Isa, his wife, to whom the diary is directed] will find a statement of my last wishes. They date from the months immediately following Marie's [their daughter's] death. . . You will find, too, my profession of faith. It runs something like this: 'Should I

1 *Genetrix*, p. 178.
2 *Angels*.
3 *Knot*.
4 *Lost*.
5 *Enemy*.

12

agree, at the moment of my death, to accept the ministrations of a priest, I herewith, while my mind remains clear, protest against the advantage that will have been taken of my weakening powers—physical as well as mental—to extort from me what my reason rejects'.[1]

But many years before this had appeared M. Roger Martin du Gard's novel, *Jean Barois* (1913); and the central theme of this novel is precisely this: should such a vow (given in almost identical terms), solemnly taken by a freethinker, be simply brushed aside when evidence of a genuine and quite conscious conversion later occurs at his death? (In fact, it is brushed aside.) Mauriac produces the same dilemma again, as a sort of anticlerical's stock-in-trade; but he leaves it lying on the page, never refers to it again, and later appears to have forgotten all about it.

However, there is perhaps a special reason why Mauriac may be allowed a little more liberty than others in treating of these themes: that he is not, in the usual sense, a 'convert'. No doubt as a child at home, and then under the Marist fathers, he developed an excessive scrupulosity. But the regular *examen* and weekly confession gave the novelist an insight into the self which (to say the least) would be effectively turned outward later.

> My first communion remained the event which dominated my life. During the months of preparation for it I had acquired a taste for perfection. M. Maysonnave, the senior curate, had sent me a book, sumptuously bound, which was a moral account book: each day I had to mark down the number of victories I'd won over my besetting sin, all my prayers, and all the merits I'd acquired by them. During the retreat I had three days of agony. I tortured myself with thoughts of death and eternity, with my general confession and with sins vaguely specified.[2]

This is a reminiscence of Jacques, the hero of Mauriac's second novel, which appeared in 1914; but there is no doubt that it is a piece of the author's autobiography. However, we must be clear that this pious childhood was not all gloom.

---

1 *Knot*, p. 111.
2 *Robe*, p. 21f.

Why was I a sad child? It would be silly to blame religion for it: it gave me more joy than pain in those days. What was it but the scruples with which I tormented myself to pay back for the emotional delights of the great Feasts ... Far from religion casting a shadow over my childhood, it enriched it with a pathetic joy. It is not because of it, but in spite of it, that I was a sad child, for I loved Christ, and He consoled me.[1]

Later, it is true, Mauriac tended to condemn this sweet-toothed piety of his youth. In 1927 he wrote a preface to a new edition of his collection of early verse, *Les Mains Jointes:*

The truth is that what I dislike in this little book is not its technique but above all its spirit. This cowardly, terrified adolescence, turned in on itself—I repudiate it now. Not that I deny my faith at that period, any more than I deny my poetry; but my manner of believing was worth about as much as my manner of verse-writing; oh, the facility of it! A child who is scared of everything sniffs incense, gets an emotion from the sacraments and enjoyment from the ritual...[2]

This was the point in his career when Mauriac was re-examining the relationship between his faith and his vocation as a writer, and the next year saw what has sometimes been described as his 'conversion'. By this is meant an act of deference to his Catholic critics, and, resulting from that, a more conscious and specific use of his talent in the cause of the Faith. But it should not be exaggerated. He may have written his *Bonheur du Chrétien* in answer to those who said that the earlier *Souf-frances du Chrétien* was too negative; but it was his journalistic and critical work rather than his novels that were immediately affected.[3] As Mr North says,

The man had taken a great step forward in the knowledge of his faith. The writer, however, changes but little. The same bitter version of the world persists in his writing, and though he avoids certain subjects now, it would be difficult to see him as an apologist for the faith, an author convinced of the goodness of man. This very real aspect of his thought

[1] *Commencements*, pp. 22-4.
[2] Quoted in du Bos, p. 46.
[3] See North, p. 63.

will find its expression in his essays on religious subjects, in his newspaper comments, but hardly in his novels.[1]

And perhaps even his condemnation of his youthful piety has to be modified slightly in view of a still later, indeed quite recent, pronouncement. In July 1951 he spoke at the prize-giving in his old school, Grand-Lebrun, and said that he owed it a great debt:

> The poetic state which is the state of childhood is most often contaminated, soiled by real life, by the horrible and hard life of grown-ups. I don't think badly of the education which French boys get in the *lycées*. I even think highly of it . . . But a pupil of Grand-Lebrun, at least in my time, was marvellously shielded, protected from the corrupt and criminal world: a catholic college like Grand-Lebrun, behind its high walls, under the trees of its enchanted gardens, in the silence of its chapel, preserves this pure water of childhood which collects there as in a very deep well. This well, on which I have never ceased to draw during my life as a writer, has not yet dried up after so many years.[2]

There is another aspect of Mauriac's general development that should be mentioned at this stage, since it belongs only incidentally to a criticism of his own work as a novelist, but is none the less revealing: his appreciation of and reaction to other writers. I think he is making no false boast when he says of himself, writing in 1938:

> I feel myself to be less unjust to-day towards the living and the dead than I used to be at twenty . . . I feel that I am now a long way from the simplicity of my youth which made me damn people with lightheartedness . . . The mystery of the judgements of God on each one of us in particular is the very mystery of pity.[3]

He is actually speaking of Renan, on whom he now passes a gentler verdict than earlier; but it would apply to his judgement on others too. Even of Gide he sometimes writes in a way which suggests genuine disinterested appreciation rather than (as,

1 North, p. 77.
2 Speech printed in *La Table Ronde*, Aug. 1951.
3 *Journal*, pp. 348-50.

alas, seems the case at other times) a forced attempt to be fair growing out of professional Christian charity. What is more surprising is his apparently warm and sincere admiration for D. H. Lawrence. It is true that he does not show very much understanding of Lawrence. And Gide was rightly annoyed by his musings about *Lady Chatterley's Lover:*

> In twenty years, or thirty [wrote Mauriac], what will Lady Chatterley do with her game-keeper? Will they continue the same gesture till death? When satiety comes, in their old age, they will seek elsewhere for a means of nourishing a lust which they have always exercised so skilfully that it is bound to go on dominating them even in their final decrepitude. I think of that terrible book: *The Old Age of Lady Chatterley.*[1]

Gide expostulates: 'If I have any remorse today, it is indeed for not having taken better advantage of my youth'.[2] Neither he nor Mauriac, of course, was aware that Lawrence himself foresaw this sort of objection ('Old people can have a lovely quiescent sort of sex, like apples.')[3] Still, it is interesting to find Mauriac writing a preface to a French translation of Lawrence's *Boy in the Bush*[4] (what a choice!) and to find him noting in his diary:

> Dear Lawrence, with Catherine Mansfield, my best English friends! I don't understand or love the English till they are dead . . . This Lawrence: I swear that I met him one day at Daniel Halévy's . . . I remember death visibly written on his drawn face, from which one averted one's eyes out of delicacy . . . Was it him? . . . It's so sad to think that I could have said to him: 'We are as far away from each other as two writers of the same age could possibly be. And yet, dear Lawrence, I admire you, I know all about you, I love you.'[5]

On the other hand—and it will already be clear from the above—Mauriac is, like so many French critics, extremely personal in his literary judgements. It is true that he sees clearly,

[1] *Journal*, p. 110.
[2] Gide: *Journal* (E.T., vol. iii, p. 359), 9th Aug. 1937.
[3] Lawrence: *Letters*, ed. Huxley, p. 773.
[4] Pref. to *Jack dans la brousse*, tr. Lilian Brach (Gallimard, 1938).
[5] *Journal*, pp. 152-4.

at least in theory, that writers like Racine, Corneille, and so on, should be judged on their works—by contrast with those like Rousseau, Voltaire, Chateaubriand, whose works we forget, but remember the man.[1] But in practice Mauriac's criticism is of the kind that can be suitably given such titles as *Mes Grands Hommes*, 'Writers in my life' . . . etc. And the result is inevitably that, in spite of occasional and almost accidental moments of genuine detached critical insight, we are mostly conscious of arbitrary and unrelated judgements; sometimes indeed, we must think, of sheer misjudgements. In a little (and little-known) book on the Catholic novelist and biographer, René Bazin,[2] Mauriac can be seen defending a second-rate writer because, one suspects, his critical theory demands that he be considered first-rate:

> Bazin has always shown himself compassionate towards the humble heroes of his books. It is certain that no trace remains in this novelist of the implacability characteristic of the French naturalists of the last century, who despise the human being—the human beast, as they call him—and who only pause from hating man when they want to mock him . . . M. René Bazin has contrived to see what greater men have not: the action of Grace in the world. He has been in a sense more naturalistic than Flaubert, Maupassant and Zola, because he has gone below the surface of beings. For him the drama of the creature is not confined to the conflict of instincts . . . Let us above all admire the way he introduces God into the most human drama. Whereas so many have failed to see this perilous enterprise through, and find themselves daily accused of scandalously mixing up the divine with the fleshly, the author of *Donatienne* and *Le Roi des Archers* brings off this *tour de force* in each of his books, perhaps with too great ease.[3]

But the qualification in this last phrase comes too late to save the passage. We shall have to bear it in mind when, in our third chapter, we discuss Mauriac's own attempts to 'introduce God into the human drama'. Meanwhile, one cannot but feel that this is not so much objective literary criticism as self-defence. Whatever may be said theoretically in favour of the

[1] *Journal*, p. 430f.
[2] *René Bazin* (ed. 'Les Quarante', Alcan, 1931).
[3] Op. cit., p. 10f.

theological type of criticism here implied, a serious critic could not speak in the same paragraph about Flaubert and the author of *Oberlé*. And the self-defence comes out even more crudely in Mauriac's concluding remarks on Bazin:

> His reward today lies in the certainty he can have that he has never upset a single one of these little ones who believe in Christ, that he has not to give an account of a single scandal, but that on the contrary he has helped a great number towards salvation. What joy and peace an artist must experience in the evening of his life, when he possesses the assurance that no soul has ever been wounded by him![1]

How Mauriac comes by criteria such as this for assessing the work of an artist can partly be seen in the background we have tried to sketch. How his own works come out of an assessment of the same nature we shall not directly discuss (though it will be implied in later chapters) since we do not accept the validity of these criteria. But already we can see that the permanent problem of Mauriac's own literary career, as well as the general problem of relating literary to theological (or, worse, to homiletic) assessment, lies behind this naïve paragraph.

II

Scope and Limits

Scope

In a brief study it is impossible to outline or analyse all the novels (still less the plays as well); nor is it necessary, since most of the important novels are easily accessible in English. But a delineation of the breadth of Mauriac's canvas is worth keeping in mind as the background to an analysis of some representative works. If we dwell longer upon the early works than they really merit, it is because they have not been, and are not likely to be, translated into English, and they do confirm what the more famous novels suggest about Mauriac's particular gifts and preoccupations.

The first novel of all, *L'Enfant Chargé de Chaînes*, gives us the education of a young Mauriac; Jean-Paul Johannet is brought

[1] *René Bazin*, p. 30.

up at a pious school, becomes interested in the young Catholic Social movement, and tries to put social theory into practise by befriending, in a self-conscious and ungainly way, a working-class boy called Georges Élie; the experiment fails, and the novel ends desultorily with Jean-Paul's first love-affair. There is nothing much in the book, but there are hints of a power to create 'atmosphere' which will be stronger as time goes on. There are also embarrassing apostrophes to the characters, or to God, in which the author intrudes blunderingly upon the scene—a weakness which, as we shall see, he never outgrows. Here, for instance, is his encouraging chat to the heroine, Marthe Balzon, who has fallen in love with Jean-Paul—they are the closing words of the novel:

> At this very same hour you, Martha, were sitting on your bed in a large room in the country . . . On the mantelpiece, in the light of the lamp, you had left Jean-Paul's last letters lying, too. Their tender and passionate words had awoken in you the joy that you expected no longer. You are smiling bravely, Martha, at all his possible betrayals: you absolve them all in advance; your meticulous love foresees, as its future revenge, a redoubling of tenderness— and the serenity of silent acts of forgiveness.[1]

Next appears *La Robe Prétexte*, which does not carry us much further, but does introduce us to the devout bourgeoisie (the governess, the nun-companion, the diplomatic, tea-drinking Abbé) and to the stock contrasts in worldly men (the would-be-rakish uncle and the father, an artist now dead) all of which will reappear in later novels. The clandestine correspondence, too, between the hero, Jacques, and Camille, a girl at a convent school, which is intercepted and stopped by the interfering Mme de Vatémesnil, is merely a foreshadowing of the similar attempt by Jean de Mirbel to communicate with Michèle, successfully foiled by Brigitte Pian.[2] *La Chair et le Sang* can equally be ignored; and *Le Fleuve de Feu* merely pursues once more the stream of first passion: this time in a girl, Gisèle de Plailly, who escapes from her guardian and follows the young man—and the grand romantic tradition—to 'the banal décor of a hotel bedroom in the Pyrenees'[3]; she is last seen praying in the church

---

[1] *L'Enfant*, pp. 273-5.
[2] *Pharisees*.
[3] Hourdin, pp. 44-5.

of a little village where she had taken refuge. There are also three little tales which follow soon after, and which begin to be characteristic of Mauriac's bitter vision. They appear collected together as *Trois Récits* in 1929: *Coups de Couteau*, *Un Homme de Lettres*, and *Le Démon de la Connaissance*; but the first was actually written three years earlier. Here we have a husband who knows his wife so well that he can, in bed, ask her advice about a failing love-affair he has with another woman—and who retains his wife's affection, or at least her pity, precisely by being made to suffer by this lover! We have the artist who is so stifled by his wife's admiration that he goes off and lives in dirt and discomfort with a woman who has two sickly and noisy brats—but later returns, having tried this experiment only to get 'copy'. Finally we have the boy who loses his faith in God, and therefore in creatures too. The second of these three tales is worth pausing over, since it gives us a character who does not occur in any other of the novels (and perhaps not in life, either), and who evidently represents a problem, cast in fictional form, for the author. Jérome is a writer who pours so much of his experience into his books that he has no sincerely personal life left. He had boasted that he had left his wife Gabrielle because

> the love which a woman has for us is not a wall behind which to take shelter; it's an obstacle to be overcome . . . And then, to create, we must have some semblance of solitude. Bertha, occupied with her children, often forgets me altogether. I was the whole of life for Gabrielle. However hard she tried to efface herself beside me, I heard her thinking of me. I have only written a single poem during the fifteen years of our liaison.[1]

But he soon belies this by leaving Bertha, and she declares that all along he was only using her as fodder for literature. Even at the supreme moment of passion he is taking notes for a novel:

> I will bury this booty [he says to himself] as a dog does a bone; I shall find it again one day, but so mingled with my own creatures that I shan't even recognise it.[2]

And when the 'I' of the story tells Jérome what he is really like, Jérome merely seizes this analysis of his own character with avidity, remarking:

[1] *Récits*, p. 117.
[2] Ibid., p. 129.

That'll be a beautiful conclusion to my obituary. It is an interesting statement, and not wholly unconvincing, of the personal problem of the compatibility of a writer's belief and behaviour with his métier.

Meanwhile by now Mauriac had begun on the well-known novels; indeed, the first, *A Kiss for the Leper*, appeared as early as 1922. From then on we have a steady succession of tales, giving us the lives of provincial folk, broken marriages, possessive mothers, sordid love-affairs, analyses of most of the possible human motives, and occasional flashes of grace. Frequent satire there is, occasional near-cynicism, but never humour. The range is evidently narrow, and when Mauriac tries to widen it by describing the fast town set, the lovers and gigolos and painted beauties that he sometimes seems to find necessary to his plots, he always and obviously fails. When, for instance, Fanny unexpectedly meets Fabien in Venice—she in company with the unconvincing ballet dancer Cyrus Bergues and his Swedish impresario, Donald Larsen—we are told:

> She raised her face to his, careless of the danger she ran in thus displaying its mask of paint and powder in the harsh light of the hotel hall. But tears had seamed the mask and broken its surface.[1]

Or here is Denis Revolou, on the subject of his sister Rose:

> He was devoured with impatience to have a look at Rose's dress ... It would, he supposed, be like all dance-frocks— frankly immodest ... In less than an hour's time she would be standing in a drawing-room doorway, offering to the common gaze the spectacle of her throat and shoulders, of her back, and even of those childish breasts that were set a shade too high. She would allow herself to be clasped, thus stripped, in the arms of the first man who might care to ask her for a dance.[2]

Are not these (and they are not merely early writings: they were written in 1924 and 1939 respectively) the stock pictures, the reactions of one for whom the town can never be anything but a mystery, superficially observed and then described in

[1] *Enemy*, p. 203.
[2] *Sea*, p. 3f.

21

clichés? The same must be said of Mauriac's attempts to present other areas of life which he only knows from a distance and at a surface level. Here, for instance, is a psychiatrist's wife on the subject of her husband, Elis. She has been eavesdropping, and has heard part of a patient's (Thérèse's) long, rambling, incoherent confession, through the door of her husband's consulting-room. She is half sorry for Thérèse, for, she muses:

> Elis was quite incapable of understanding her, even of feeling compassion for her. All he would do, as he had done with other victims, was to urge her to find relief—to free her emotions through the gratification of the body. That was what his method amounted to. The same filthy key served him whether it was heroism, crime, sanctity or renunciation he had to interpret.[1]

And we cannot say that this is merely subtle 'thinking in character', for it is the sheerest caricature, not merely of the work of a psychiatrist, but of a possible judgement from a psychiatrist's wife; and unfortunately the style shows us that it is Mauriac's own view sneaking in.

As if half-aware that, with the failure of these attempts to widen its scope, his repertoire was beginning to run out, Mauriac in 1938 turned to the stage. This is not, admittedly, his own account of the experiment. What he says is:

> An author is often accused of never renewing himself. I believe on the contrary that his first duty is to remain himself, to accept his limitations. It is excellent for a novelist to submit himself to constraints which he has not known before. I don't believe in the incompatibility that is so often alleged between the gifts of a novelist and those of a dramatist. There is no reason why the characters we create should not be able to assume a body and a voice . . This same desire to discover a new mode of expression inclines me to reserve the future for matters concerned with the cinema . . . [But] the exacting technique of the theatre, exacting because of the multiple problems it poses, the obstacles which it ranges in front of one, seems to me to be a better school for the artist than that of the screen.[2]

1 *Thérèse*, p. 134.
2 *Journal*, pp. 369-371.

Mauriac has on the whole shown great skill in adapting himself to this theatrical technique. But skill is one thing, dramatic success another. The unreal figure, for instance, of Blaise Coutûre in *Asmodée* seems to me a melodramatic projection of what Mauriac imagines a priest *manqué* ought to turn out like in the circumstances of a country family house: he is the product of a formula. Could any speech be less convincing than this of Coutûre's:

> Of all the creatures upon whom I have acted there isn't one whom I haven't first of all inspired with aversion. Emmanuèle? But I only ask you for three days in which to make her see only through my eyes, make no gesture that isn't inspired by me, and in which my will may be substituted for hers and command even the beating of her heart.[1]

Of course no man, even if he were like that in fact, would speak like that of himself. Clearly it is the author speaking from the wings while he twitches the strings of the marionette. We shall see the extent to which this also happens in the novels; but in a play it is even more fatal, for a flaw of this sort cannot on the stage be concealed behind a curtain of descriptive prose. And the plays that have followed since, though again skilful in their way, cannot be said to have enabled Mauriac to bring precision to his particular talent, still less to enlarge his range. Indeed, perhaps they have helped to reveal a weakness that is native to him. He has recognised himself that his novels are successful in part 'thanks to a certain gift of atmosphere'.[2] And there is no doubt that the effectiveness of most of his scenes is due, as we shall see in the last chapter, to the atmospheric background against which they are played—the sighing of the pines, the morose silence of the marshes, the croaking of frogs. Deprived of this, his dramatic experiments have had to rely on the naked interplay of character and motive, and the author is too easily tempted to supplement this bareness by working into them the comment which either should never be made from outside at all, or at least be reserved for the narrator and not tacked on to the dialogue within the play.

And if, finally, we are to some extent to judge Mauriac's range by bringing the examination of his works as nearly up to date as possible, it cannot be said, unfortunately, that the

1 *Asmodée*, p. 177f.
2 *Journal*, p. 218.

long-short stories to which he has returned recently show us that his excursion into the theatre has effected a renewal of creativity. In *The Little Misery* there is a touching enough picture of the snotty, wizened little *sagouin*, a picture which shows, perhaps, something more of pity and less of disgust than, for instance, Mauriac's earlier picture of the young Jean Péloueyre with his 'ferrety face', his 'miserable undeveloped body, untouched by the normal miracle of puberty'.[1] And we can add that the slight sketch of the pleasant, kindly marxist schoolmaster is unusually objective. But the melodramatic conclusion—the suicide of father and son in the millrace—is arbitrary and unconvincing. *Galigaï*, too, repeats several old formulae, though the central character, Mme Agathe ('Galigaï') who loses young Nicolas Plassac and gains instead the old widower, Armand Dubernet, is well presented. It is significant that the author seems to see the story as the education of Nicolas, whereas I think the average reader will find Nicolas shadowy and uninteresting and Galigaï herself the real centre; significant, because Mauriac constantly misjudges his own operations, and the misjudgement reveals a fundamental uncertainty in the writer which can be detected in the handling of the novels themselves. It is, of course, within the creation that the creator's weaknesses are seen. To that creation, in more detail, we therefore now turn.

Limits

(i) The most obvious, though not the most important, indications of a writer's limitations are to be found in his repetitions. There is a repetition that makes for strength—that spiral development which like a fugue uses repetition precisely to build up. But there is also a repetition that is mere tautology. Sometimes Mauriac's repetitions are spiral, as when he tries out a character like Mme de Blénauge,[2] and then realises her more fully in a Brigitte Pian;[3] or an Yves Frontenac[4] whom he expands (though also with some loss of freshness) into Pierre Costadot[5]—Pierre is allowed to quote the poetry which Yves merely wrote. But often there are similarities between characters

---

[1] *Leper*, p. 15.
[2] *Lost*.
[3] *Pharisees*.
[4] *Frontenac*.
[5] *Sea*.

which suggest that Mauriac is merely falling back on a convenient pattern, e.g. the unknown priest to whom Mme de Blénauge confesses, the young Abbé Alain Forcas, to whom Mathilde Desbats (and later Gabriel Gradère) confess,[1] the Jesuit to whom Lucienne Revolou makes an unsatisfactory confession before her last illness,[2] the young priest whose solitude Thérèse understands and sympathises with,[3] and finally, of course the Abbé Calou who brings peace to the soul of Brigitte Pian. And if it is replied that the very impersonality of the priest rightly makes the appearance of a standard repetitive pattern inevitable, we can point to other types—to the stagey villains who appear at the right moments to provide appropriate temptations (usually sexual); to the faithful peasant retainers who hover at the foot of stairs; to the weak, bewildered, often asthmatic or dyscardiac fathers-in-law whose vegetable existence occasionally stirs into violent eruption. Apart from close verbal echoes (like the account of the children's game of making whistles from apricot stones, which appears almost word-for-word in *Le Mystère Frontenac*[4] and *Woman of the Pharisees*[5]) there are some striking repetitions which M. Joseph Majault has listed for us.[6] In *Woman of the Pharisees*, *Le Mystère Frontenac* and *Desert of Love* a man, affected by congestion of the lungs, dies beside his mistress. In *Dark Angels*, *Le Mystère Frontenac* and *Thérèse* there are identical descriptions of a station with saw-mills and resinous planks stacked near-by. In *L'Enfant Chargé de Chaînes* and *La Chair et le Sang* occurs the same sentence: 'un peu de valenciennes paraît dans l'entrebâillement du corsage'. All little girls in the novels appear to have sturdy legs and low, broad rumps; many of the women have bilious-looking faces, but broad, often enormous, foreheads.

(ii) Such careless echoes would not matter, if there did not go with them an uneasiness in the actual handling. We have suggested that Mauriac too often helps himself out by importing, from outside his own experience, stock incidents or characters which can get him round the next corner of his plot. Let us examine some examples. The young doctor in *A Kiss for the Leper* is obviously injected into the book merely to test Noémie's

[1] *Angels.*
[2] *Sea.*
[3] *Thérèse*, p. 67.
[4] P. 43.
[5] P. 7.
[6] Majault, pp. 108-10, and cf. pp. 153-4.

loyalty to Jean Péloueyre's memory; what we are told of him is totally unconvincing:

> He had elongated eyes like an Andalusian mule, and he turned them boldly on Noémie, tracing the lines of her body with a lingering thoroughness ... The medical talk came strangely from lips better suited to dispense kisses than scientific comments.[1]

> His mind was busy with Noémie. There she was, within reach of his hand, yet he never touched her. 'All the same', said the sportsman in him, 'I've winged her: she's wounded'. He knew instinctively when a female victim had been brought to bay and was begging for mercy. He had heard the cry of her young body. He had possessed many women—some, forbidden fruit; some, the wives of men and not discarded bits of rubbish like that wretched Péloueyre. Winged now, and less capable of resistance than most, was she to be his only failure?[2]

If it be said that this piece of novelettish villainy belongs after all to a fairly early work (1922), then we must set beside it another from *Woman of the Pharisees*, written nearly twenty years later. It describes how a pious schoolmistress, who was under the Abbé Calou's care, gets under the evil influence of one Hortense Voyod,

> a type of amazon not wholly unknown, contrary to general opinion, in country districts. There are people who set their toils and are prepared to go hungry for a very long while before any prey lets itself be caught. The patience of vice is infinite. One single victim will content such people, and a brief moment of contact will ensure them long years of happy repletion.[3]

Two things have gone wrong here. First, the whole incident, even the existence of the otherwise irrelevant, and never clearly visualised, schoolmistress, is only introduced to show the Abbé Calou's sanctity, and resulting unpopularity: it has, therefore, the unreality of a chess-move. And second, the author

[1] P. 74f.
[2] P. 85.
[3] *Pharisees*, p. 153f.

26

having failed to get a clear picture of the villainess in his mind, has tried the dodge of putting her over for us by means of a long-drawn-out and hazy entomological metaphor. But what we are left with is no precise conception of her, but only the vague evocation of a 'spider-and-fly' cliché.

Unfortunately this kind of unreality tends even to invade the central characters. Since *Woman of the Pharisees* has been widely proclaimed as Mauriac's masterpiece, let us take Brigitte Pian herself. As I hope to show later, the conversion or transformation of Brigitte seems to me excellently done. But it is at a cost: the cost of an over-drawn, sometimes even incredible, picture of the earlier Brigitte. When the boy who tells the story, Louis, discovers the love-affair between Octavia Tronche and M. Puybaraud, and is longing to reveal it to his step-mother, Brigitte, this conversation occurs:

> 'Mother', I said, 'there's something I want to tell you. But'— I added with a touch of hypocrisy—'I'm not sure whether I ought.'
>
> 'My dear child' [replies Brigitte], 'I have no idea what you have to say. But there is one rule which you would do well to follow blindly, and that is, never to keep anything from your second mother. For on her has devolved the duty of bringing you up.'
>
> 'Even when it is a secret involving others?'
>
> 'If it involves others that is all the more reason why you should tell me', she replied sharply.[1]

I frankly do not believe Brigitte would have found that in her books of piety and moral theology; still less would she state it thus bluntly. Later, having pursued and persecuted poor M. Puybaraud and Octavia, now his wife, Brigitte is shown to us bewailing their ingratitude and speaking, again to her step-son, these unlikely words:

> I sometimes wonder, dear child, whether I don't give too much of myself when I work for the salvation of my neighbours. Oh, I know that the least among them is of infinite worth. I would give my life that one might be saved. But there are moments when I am frightened to think how much time I have wasted (at least, it *seems* wasted, but of that God alone is judge) over insignificant, nay, evil persons. It is the cross

[1] Op. cit., p. 17.

27

laid upon the great-hearted that they shall exhaust themselves in darkness and uncertainty on behalf of the spiritually mean and inferior.[1]

Finally, when she has got Puybaraud and Octavia into her financial clutches, and the defenceless Octavia is threatened with a miscarriage, if not with worse, Brigitte with an unbelievable complacency excuses herself for endangering her life by revealing the worst to the unsuspecting pregnant woman, thus:

> She might [she said of herself] have been weak enough to yield to his [Puybaraud's] representations [that she should spare Octavia by concealing bad news from her] had she been dealing with one of those worldly persons . . . who know nothing of the ways of God. But she had decided that a Christian like Octavia ought not to remain ignorant of the consequences of her acts, that she ought to face the trials which Providence had seen fit to lay upon her. 'Since it was already part of the Divine plan that you should live on the charity of a devoted friend, and that M. Puybaraud should be unable to find suitable employment in the work-aday world, I felt that I had no right to spare you the effects of so salutary a lesson.[2]

What one feels about all these three passages is that they have been simply 'cooked'; that for the sake of the enlightenment that is to come to Brigitte, movingly, at the end of the book, we must be allowed to see her in an arbitrarily imposed blackness beforehand. And the reason this carries no conviction is that a woman as subtly cruel and self-satisfied as she is thus supposed to be would be too intelligent to reveal her arrogance by talking, especially talking to a boy, as Brigitte is here made to do. One more instance of this sheer failure in imagination comes from what I believe to be in many ways his best novel, *Le Mystère Frontenac*. Yves is talking to his girl-friend, his 'pick-up', in Paris, soon after he has had the bitter experience of the death of the Frontenac children's 'Uncle Xavier'—the experience that ultimately jolts Yves out of the life he is living at this moment.

> While he was talking, she powdered and rouged her face. When he told her about the death of Uncle Xavier, she asked

[1] Op. cit., p. 58.
[2] P. 126f.

distractedly whether he was an uncle who had anything to leave.

'He had given us practically all he had' [replies Yves], 'while he was still alive.'

'Oh well; then his death is no longer of much interest.'[1]

Now, this would be all very well in a novel by Miss Ivy Compton-Burnett, where the whole technique (and the whole fun) consists in making characters improbably say exactly what they are thinking. But in Mauriac's semi-realistic technique it is really a shocking misjudgement.

(iii) I have used the phrase 'semi-realistic technique'; and I think as a matter of fact that a further weakness in Mauriac's novels lies in his uncertainty what technique to adopt. He himself admired James Joyce's and Virginia Woolf's use of the 'interior monologue', which, he says, is so suitable for expressing 'this immense, tangled world, always changing, always motionless, which we call a single human consciousness'.[2] And Mauriac often uses this monologue to considerable effect. But sometimes he mixes it with other elements that do not marry. At one point he is even so jejune as to raise the difficulty and defend himself within the novel itself. The narrator, Louis, in *Woman of the Pharisees*, says:

> Someone will be sure to ask: 'But how do you know so much about events of which you were not a witness? What right have you to reproduce conversations which you cannot have heard?' Well, if the truth must be told, I have outlived most of my characters, several of whom played an important part in my life. Besides, I am the sort of man who keeps old papers, and I have at my disposal not only a private diary [Monsieur Puybaraud's], but various notes made by Monsieur Calou which Mirbel found after the priest's death.[3]

Mauriac would have done better never to raise the question. As it is he has now to make the unconvincing attempt to adjust the rest of the narrative to the availability of the evidence—though fortunately for the tale he does not always remember to do so.

Another flaw in technique is I think the overlapping, so to

1 *Frontenac*, p. 268.
2 *Le Romancier et ses personnages*, p. 117f., quot. Majault, p. 243.
3 Op. cit., p. 33.

speak, of two time-sequences. This is particularly marked when Mauriac gives us a sudden 'flash-forward' into the future. We have quoted an example already—the end of his first novel, *L'Enfant Chargé de Chaînes*.[1] A clearer, and really more disturbing instance occurs, twice over, in *Le Mystère Frontenac*. José, the 'bad boy' of the family, has been very obstinate towards Blanche Frontenac, the mother of the family; and it has taken Jean-Louis, the older brother, to bring him to his senses:

> The two brothers came towards her.
> 'He'll be sensible now, Mother, [says Jean-Louis], 'he's promised me.'
> She drew José towards her, to kiss him, poor unhappy child.
> 'Darling, you won't ever put on that expression again, will you?'
> He would put it on again once more, this terrible expression, several years later, on the evening of a lovely clear, warm day, towards the end of August 1915, at Mourmelon, between two bivouac camps. No one would pay any attention to it, not even his companion, who was just reassuring him: 'It looks as if there's going to be a thundering great artillery preparation—they'll all be laid flat; we'll have nothing to do but advance with slung rifles, our hands in our pockets . .' José Frontenac would look at him with the same expression, empty of all hope—but which on this day will frighten nobody.[2]

And the same flash-forward happens again later. Yves has just heard from Joséfa, Uncle Xavier's mistress, that old Xavier is very ill with angina. When she has gone, he throws himself on the couch, and thinks back to his family days.

> 'Mother!' he sobbed, 'Mother . . .'
> The tears came. He was the first of the Frontenac children to call on their dead mother as if she was still alive. Eighteen months later, it would be José's turn to do it, his stomach gashed open, for a whole interminable night in September, between two trenches.[3]

This way of settling the fate of a character in a few lines by

1 Vide sup., p. 19.
2 Op. cit., p. 172f.
3 Ibid., p. 243.

prophetic prediction is always dangerous in the novel, but more so when it represents the superimposition of one technique upon another.

Sometimes Mauriac's uncertainty is less obtrusive; it is betrayed by a clumsy arrangement of unlikely coincidence, which is always the sign of a failure to make a genuine *internal* relation between events. For instance, after Gabriel Gradère has dropped every conceivable melodramatic hint of his intending murder of someone (either Symphorien Desbats or his mistress, Aline) he goes to intercept Aline when she arrives by train, with intent to lead her off into the waste ground and there do away with her. At this moment Alain Forcas, the priest, is praying in his room, with Gradère's confessional note-book open before him.

> The rain fell harder. He told himself that it was rustling with just the same sound on the roof of the chateau of Liogats, where in one of the rooms the poor soul who had covered these pages with scrawled writing was lying asleep ... At that moment, he had an almost physical sense of the co-inherence of human souls, of that mysterious union in which we are all of us involved alike by sin and grace. He wept for very love of sinners. The whistle of a train came to his ears through the darkness. The wheels of a long line of trucks rumbled over the rails. The noise of escaping steam filled the air. He thought: 'That must be the nine-o'clock just running into the station.' Why should the arrival of that particular train have any meaning for him? Suddenly a load of sadness descended upon his spirit with so crushing a weight that he leaned his head upon the table. His forehead touched the thin blue book.[1]

This seems to me admirably to illustrate Mauriac's strength and weakness: the strength in the conveyance of spiritual oppression, the weakness in the artificial arrangement of the situation. Who, in fact, says the words: 'Why should the arrival of that particular train have any meaning for him?' If it is the priest's own premonition of trouble, it is too far-fetched. But if not, then it can only be Mauriac's own question, inserted *ab extra*: and this at once disturbs the flow of the novel.

Another exhibition of uncertainty of handling occurs when Mauriac requires an incident or experience to happen to one

[1] *Angels*, p. 285.

31

of his characters, but, in default of clear visualisation of it, tries to hint at a vast expanse in a hazy paragraph. Roger North considers that the end of *Woman of the Pharisees* is a failure because the doctor, Gellis, with whom Brigitte falls in love at a late age and who teaches her the meaning of human affection, is only introduced hurriedly in the last seven pages. He considers that if Mauriac had ended with the death, sad but triumphant, of the Abbé Calou, and with Brigitte's humiliation, it would have been more plausible and more effective.[1] There is truth in this, though I do not find the failure of technique so serious here as elsewhere, because it is redeemed by the last pages of the book. A better example of this brusque skating-over a difficult passage occurs at the end of *The Unknown Sea*. After Pierre Costadot ('Pierrot') has been nearly involved in the sudden death of the family's former lawyer, Landin, he 'goes wild' in Paris:

> The only way [thought Pierrot] to make a beginning was to come to grips with fallen human nature and its morbid growths. But this wretchedness of man's estate, this wound in the soul which might once have prompted his religious instincts to find a solution in the mysteries of faith, worked now in an opposite direction . .

He takes a mistress; but this phase of life is indicated in the vaguest of generalisations and moralisations:

> He could never get rid of the feeling that virtue was going out of him. Argue as he might, he could not but be convinced that all his satisfactions led to death. The filthy sewage of the world was in his eyes and nose, his ears and mouth. He lived in a constant state of spiritual agony, unable to endure the very pleasures which had become more necessary to him than bread and wine.[2]

And so on. The whole episode is over in three pages, and is brought to an end by Pierre reading a book recently published by Renan's grandson, and also Péguy's *Mystère de la Charité de Jeanne d'Arc*. This is very edifying, no doubt; but it is not novel-writing.

If we look closer I think we shall find that the trouble in all

1 North, p. 89.
2 Op. cit., pp. 187, 189.

these passages lies in a failure of *attention*. When we hear a singer falter and her notes become uncertain and forced, we know that she has forgotten the song itself and is thinking of her diaphragm or breath-control. Sometimes this kind of self-consciousness comes out into the open in Mauriac. The well-known preface to *The End of the Night*, in which he explains that he had original-ly written the description of Thérèse's death-bed reconciliation, but had destroyed it because he could not visualise the priest who would hear her confession—this we must respect for its transparent honesty. And perhaps even the charming preface to *Trois Récits*, which contains a similar self-exculpation, is too ingenuous for anyone to quarrel with:

> 'To offer oneself, by means of humiliations, to the coming of inspirations': the most beautiful tale of this collection, and the one which ought to have this *Pensée* of Pascal's as its *exergum*, is the fourth, the one the author has not written, has not yet deserved to write.[1]

But too often we are conscious within the novel itself of the reflex attention of the author upon the process of writing. Louis, the 'I' of *Woman of the Pharisees*, occasionally exclaims: 'If I were writing a novel, I should . . .' —a well-known novelists' dodge. And once Louis claims to be suppressing some evidence he has —the correspondence between Puybaraud and Octavia:

> Not because it does not deserve publication, but because I doubt whether there are many readers capable of appreciating the charm of true humility, of that particular manifestation of humility which takes no heed of itself and seems completely ignorant of its effect on others.[2]

This is a somewhat artless attempt to divert critical attention from the author's inability to present this humility, by directing it against the pretended imperceptiveness of the public. But the crudest example of 'author's technique' called to the rescue in a difficult literary situation is the conclusion of one of Mauriac's least successful stories of passion, *The Enemy*. Fabien Dézaymeries, after a protracted love-affair with Fanny, spends a restless night wandering by the river, as a result of which he not unnaturally gets pleurisy. He nearly dies, and in that

1 *Récits*, p. xxxif.
2 Op. cit., p. 53.

33

condition he is reconciled to the Church. When he recovers, he makes the break with Fanny, and, to his pious mother's delight, destroys a letter from her unopened. There follows the conclusion of the story:

> In order that his mistress should be saved he had refused to open his heart to the call of human happiness, and already he was dead to the world. But for all his resolution the claims of the body could not be altogether stilled. For long months it had been gorged: how then, when it had once more woken to life, could it be kept from craving satisfaction? The real story of Fabien Dézaymeries should, properly speaking, begin at this point, for all that had gone before was in the nature of a prologue. But how is one to describe the secret drama of a man who struggles to subdue his earthy heritage, that drama which finds expression neither in words nor gestures? Where is the artist who may dare to imagine the processes and shifts of that great protagonist—Grace? It is the mark of our slavery and of our wretchedness that we can, without lying, paint a faithful portrait only of the passions.[1]

When a creative writer starts to justify himself for what he cannot do, we begin to doubt the effectiveness of even what he can, as the public orator who begins to anticipate possible heckling will forget the very speech he has come to deliver in his anxiety to keep the bad eggs at bay.

III

The Apologetic Novelist

To consider the familiar problem of the 'Catholic novelist' would require a separate treatise. Here we shall submit this aspect of Mauriac's work to a criticism similar to that in the last chapter, that is, a criticism of it *as writing*. This is not to subscribe to a dogma of art as 'pure form'; it is merely to say that theological or metaphysical weakness betrays itself even in style and organisation.

(i) Mauriac, especially since his 'conversion' in 1928 to 1929,[2]

[1] Op. cit., p. 279.
[2] Vide sup. p. 13, for the sense in which we use this word of him.

has found it incumbent upon him to indulge in apologetic. From the Christian point of view this is commendable, of course. We do not, for instance, forget the courageous letter he wrote to the philosopher Gabriel Marcel in 1929 ('Mais enfin, M. Marcel, pourquoi n'êtes-vous pas des nôtres?'[1]), with what the Christian must consider its important and fruitful consequences. And when he turns, as in his excellent little book *La Pierre d'Achoppement*,[2] to a serious and responsible scrutiny of the world of popular Catholic devotion and practice, he performs a most valuable task for us. But two disadvantages have accompanied this development: apologetic has frequently been replaced by apologizing; and much of the apology has had to be directed towards his own people. This latter disadvantage has been serious, in that it has induced that nervousness about his reception, that self-exculpatory anxiety, which has harmed even his creative writing. In his preface to *Trois Récits*, already cited, he tries to meet his Catholic critics:

> And so I pride myself on painting a world in revolt against the Tribunal of conscience, a miserable world, devoid of Grace, and so, without rejecting any of my freedom as a writer, to reach an indirect apology for Christianity. It is quite impossible, I said to myself, to reproduce the modern world as it exists, without displaying the violation of a holy law.[3]

As he puts it later in *Dark Angels* (it is actually Gradère, writing his confession in his diary), 'The way into the supernatural often starts from the depths'.[4] And Mauriac's own comment in the same novel, preparing us for Gradère's conversion, is:

> Did the wretched man, who had poured into this child's exercise-book all the abomination of his life, know of what good he was capable? Those who seem dedicated to evil may, perhaps, be chosen above their fellows: the very depth of their fall gives a measure of the vocation that they have betrayed. None would be blessed had they not been given the power to damn themselves. Perhaps only those are damned who might have been saints.[5]

[1] Vide G. Marcel, *Être et Avoir*, p. 29f.; R. Troisfontaines, *Existentialisme et Pensée Chrétienne* (1948), p. 33.
[2] Pub. 1951.
[3] Op. cit., p.xiv.
[4] *Angels*, p. 155.
[5] Ibid., p. 284.

In 1937 Mauriac heard a sermon from the Bishop of Mans in the church of Saint-Roch, Paris, declaiming against writers who

> on the pretext of freedom of inspiration, actually claim to be able to reconcile audacious descriptions and paintings with the practice of the sacraments . . . These men pride themselves on being pious while they trouble and pervert others.[1]

Mauriac is relieved to learn later that he was not meant to be included in this condemnation—that, indeed, Monsignor Grente enjoyed his novels. But it drove him to a further attempt to defend the Catholic novelist.[2] He manages, by great self-control, even to accept the action of a Catholic review for *bien-pensants*, which listed his play *Asmodée* under the heading: 'For informed adults who for certain reasons (e.g. for a family party) cannot in a particular circumstance refuse to go to the theatre'. In this defence Mauriac repeats the old theme, that a writer's works 'can have no other essence than corrupted nature, since they take their origin from there and since even the least impure of them are always born of this corruption'.[3] And finally, as recently as December 1951, Mauriac found himself still having to meet the same criticism from within the fold.

> At the moment of publishing *Galigaï* I experience the same disquiet as thirty years ago when one of my books was born; the fear not, admittedly, of scandalizing, but of disconcerting those of my readers who have religious preoccupations in common with me. The misunderstanding is shown, besides, in other circumstance than the publication of a novel. Thus, a man of religion writes to me that he has been deceived in *La Table Ronde*: my sole presence at the head of the Editorial Board had incited him to read it, and no doubt to recommend it to his young people. This Father considered it strange that I should devote time to so *useless* a periodical. There is the misunderstanding: for a man of religion, and even for a simple layman, if he is devout, to write means first of all to serve. That the artist has no other concern than to paint well and to clarify his painting, as Gide set himself to do

---

[1] *Journal*, p. 375.
[2] Ibid., p. 375f; and in expanded form in a volume of essays, *L'Homme et le Péché*, ed. Présences (Plon, 1938).
[3] *L'Homme et le Péché*, p. 218.

—this is what an 'apostle' has the utmost difficulty in conceiving.[1]

And Mauriac goes on to make some interesting observations on his own works. Re-reading them for a complete edition, he says:

> I see in many places Grace cropping up—but, it seems to me, a bit less so the older I have grown. It still emerges in a niggardly way in the last pages of *The Little Misery*. In *Galigaï*, to guess that the destiny of one of my characters points towards God you have to wait for the very last sentence, the last word.
>
> What a black picture! This deformed humanity, with its wry grimaces, which Grace has failed to get a purchase on—in favour of whom or of what does it testify? There is the Christian objection.

He has to admit that this Christian objection is powerful. In response he now says, more modestly than in earlier days, that the artist does not in fact know what he is doing as he writes. And therefore in the last resort he has to 'resign himself to having no other excuse than that of his vocation'. Is this an arrogant claim, to have such a vocation? And are there no vocations to evil too?

> Exactly! Perhaps I have been created and placed in this little canton of the universe, at a time when Rebellion is the theme on which our best minds most readily exercise themselves, only to bear witness to the guilt of man before the infinite innocence of God; and, as R. M. Albérès wrote à propos *The Little Misery*, 'to set in opposition to metaphysical literature, where man complains of everything, a psychological literature where he complains only of himself'.

This is a claim and a defence which must be acknowledged to have some validity, at least in theory. But only if they can be made good in the flesh and blood of the novels themselves. Can they?

(ii) But before we try to answer that question a little more specifically, we must remember Mauriac's apologetic directed

1 *La Table Ronde*, Dec. 1951, p. 77 (reprinted as Pref. to *Galigaï*).

outwards: for he has also to defend himself on the other flank. In 1928 Gide wrote Mauriac a letter, à propos the latter's *Life of Jean Racine*:

> You rejoice in the fact that God, before seizing hold of Racine again, left him time to write his plays, to write them *despite* his conversion. In short, what you seek is . . . permission to be a Christian without having to burn your books; and this is what makes you write them in such a way that, though a Christian, you will not have to disavow them. All this (this reassuring compromise that allows one to love God without losing sight of Mammon) . . . gives one that anguished conscience which lends such charm to your face, such savour to your writings . . . You are not sufficiently Christian to cease being a writer.[1]

It was this crude, indeed monstrous over-statement of the dilemma that prompted Mauriac to write *God and Mammon* in reply. And the controversy did not stop there. Mauriac wrote in 1931: 'Even in the state of grace my creatures are born of the murkiest part of myself'.[2] And Gide comments triumphantly in his diary, 'What a confession! This amounts to saying that if he were a perfect Christian, he would cease to have any material from which to make his novels. Is not this precisely what I told him?'[3] But once again, the matter is not so simple as Gide likes to make out. The inability of the artist to paint paradise and carry conviction is no condemnation either of paradise or of art. Mauriac observes wisely later on:

> It happens that in the presence of beings who have progressed far towards God (I think of certain little Sisters, certain novices) we are reminded of those diaphanous cocoons abandoned by the chrysalis—they seem, as it were, so emptied of themselves. The devil loses his rights (and here the devil is the novelist 'who sees everything in sable black', or an author of pitiless 'maxims' [sc. La Rochefoucauld]), the devil loses his rights over the creature who is stripped before his Creator. And that is why the novel about sanctity will never be written.[4]

---

[1] Cit., Gide, *Journal* (E.T., J. O'Brien, III, 162-3n.)
[2] *Nouvelle Revue Française*, June 1931.
[3] Gide, op. cit., p. 162.
[4] Mauriac, *Journal*, p. 54.

(iii) This brings us nearer at last to the real issue. 'The novel about sanctity will never be written'; but will even the novel about damnation be a good novel if it is too consciously and deliberately about damnation? That is the question that literary criticism will ask. And the corresponding question that theology will ask: is anyone but God qualified to write a novel about either sanctity or damnation? If anyone is in fact damned, He alone can know about it.

This is the context in which to look at the well-known accusation by M. Jean-Paul Sartre. In the *Nouvelle Revue Française* for February 1939, M. Sartre wrote on 'M. François Mauriac et la liberté'.[1] He discusses *The End of the Night* in particular, and quotes the passage about Thérèse:

> She heard nine o'clock strike. She must still find some way of killing time, for it was too early as yet to swallow the cachet which would assure her a few hours of sleep. As a rule, *though hope was dead in her, she was too proud to have recourse to drugs.* But to-night she could not resist the promise of their help.[2]

But here the translator has been kind to Mauriac, and softened the sentence to which M. Sartre takes exception. Mauriac wrote, for the sentence italicised above, 'non que ce fut dans les habitudes de cette désespérée prudente'[3]; and Sartre asks: 'who judges that Thérèse is a "désespérée prudente"? It can't be Thérèse herself. No, it is M. Mauriac, it is I myself: we have the Desqueyroux dossier in our hands, and we file our accusation'. Here, says M. Sartre, is the novelist's ambiguity in the use of the third person. Sometimes it is 'she-subject', as when the passage opens with 'She heard nine o'clock strike. She must...' Sometimes, however, it is 'she-object', when the novelist stands outside and judges her. And the trouble, M. Sartre continues, is that Mauriac before writing 'forges the essence' of his characters, decrees that they shall be this or that. Sometimes he even takes us by the hand and tips us the wink that he has done well. For instance when Mauriac says of Thérèse: 'She interrupted herself then in the middle of a sentence (for she was acting in entire good faith)...'[4] M. Sartre comments: 'I know of no

1 Reprinted in *Situations*.
2 *Night*, p. 172 (italics mine).
3 *La Fin de la Nuit*, p. 17.
4 Ibid., p. 162 (*Thérèse*, p. 246).

39

cruder artifice than this admonishing between parentheses'. And he concludes that Mauriac's great weakness is that he wishes to be God: but the novelist is not God. He describes *The End of the Night* as:

> This angular and frozen work, with bits from the theatre, bits of analysis, poetic meditations ... this motionless narrative, which exhibits its intellectual mechanism at the first glance, where the dumb ˋfigures of the heroes are inscribed like angles in a circle.

And having discussed the relation between his own existentialist conception of freedom and the freedom which a novel, and the characters within a novel, must have, he concludes that Mauriac, through the sin of pride, is not a novelist:

> He has wanted to ignore the fact—as have indeed most of our authors—that the theory of relativity applies entirely to the universe of the novel; that in a true novel there is no more room than there is in the world of Einstein for a privileged observer, and that in the system of a novel, as in a physicist's system, there exists no experience which enables one to discover whether this system is in movement or in repose. M. Mauriac has preferred himself. He has chosen the divine omniscience and omnipotence. But a novel is written by a man for men. In the sight of God, who penetrates through appearances without coming to a halt in them, there is no novel, there is no art, since art lives by appearances. God is not an artist; neither is M. Mauriac.

Critics have come to Mauriac's aid. M. Joseph Majault[1] quotes against M. Sartre some words used by Mauriac himself which show that Mauriac is not at all ignorant of the kind of issue M. Sartre is discussing. Mauriac has been saying that the novelist's difficulties in relation to his characters are like those of God in relation to man:

> In each case it is a question of reconciling the freedom of the creature and the freedom of the creator. The heroes of our novels must be free in the sense in which a theologian says that man is free; the novelist must not intervene arbitrarily

---

[1] Majault, p. 270.

in their destiny . . . But on the other hand, God also must be free, infinitely free to act on His creature.[1]

And elsewhere Mauriac has also .observed that authors are not

emulators of God—they are apes of God . . . The characters which they invent are by no means created, if creation consists in making something out of nothing.[2]

This shows us, we must agree, that M. Sartre was not saying anything very new, and that Mauriac was well aware of the problem, at least in theory. We find it difficult, though, to reconcile that awareness with Mauriac's treatment of some of his characters; for instance with his remarks about Landin, of whom he tells us, at the time of his death, that there is

. . . a frontier beyond which no human aid could be of any avail to Landin, and where no salvation on earth or in heaven awaited him . . . The unquenchable fires of hell are *lit* in this world, and those whom theologians count as lost are marked for damnation at their birth and even before it.[3]

Double predestination is neither good Catholic doctrine nor a good basis for novel-writing.

Mlle Nelly Cormeau's defence of Mauriac is even more strenuous. Her main point is that a similar 'omniscience' of the author, similar intrusions by him into his novels, and a similar 'ambiguity of the third person' can be found in passages from the most distinguished writers. She quotes passages from Balzac and Stendhal, and refers to critical writings on Flaubert, Proust, etc.[4] I cannot say that I find her parallels convincing, given the total context, technique and tone of the works from which they are taken. It would be possible, admittedly, to select from a major English novelist such as George Eliot plenty of passages in which the canon against the intrusion of 'author's comment' was infringed. But George Eliot is a different sort of novelist from Mauriac, and so are Stendhal, Flaubert, and Proust. The real weakness in the passages which M. Sartre (rightly, I believe) attacks, is this: that the transposition from 'she-subject'

1 *Le Roman*, p. 60.
2 *Le Romancier et ses Personnages*, p. 95f. (Quoted Majault, p. 61).
3 *Sea*, p. 186f.
4 Cormeau, appendix, pp. 364-380.

to 'she-object', from participatory narrative to external comment, is sudden, unprepared-for, and therefore jolting—the author himself is clearly unaware of what is happening, and the resulting jolt that he gives us betrays a loss of grip on his part.

M. Sartre's criticism depends in no wise upon his existential philosophy, but is evidence of a rather surprising acuity (surprising, when we remember the same author's curious valuation of Baudelaire and serious over-praise of William Faulkner). Let me endorse M. Sartre's point by giving some further examples of the sort of failure that he is indicating. We may divide them into two types: direct external intrusions by the author into the narrative; and internal evidence of a shift from genuine living speech and thought to a sort of ventriloquizing through his characters' mouths.

Of the first type there are many instances. Raymond Courrèges is lamenting the absence of Maria Cross, his beloved:

> He carried with him a tearing, frantic capability of passion, inherited from his father . . . There could be no hope for either of them, father or son, unless, before they died, He should reveal Himself Who, unknown to them, had drawn and summoned from the depths of their beings this burning, bitter tide.[1]

Here the author bursts frankly into the narrative, wagging an admonitory finger. Or here is an example where we see a character, first through the eyes of another character in the same novel, and then, without warning, through the author's own eyes. Fanny has appeared, and first Fabien, then gradually Mauriac, look at her:

> There she stood, her young body apparently untouched by the passing of the years, strong as steel, tempered and hardened and possessed. Sin, in its way, is a form of life. There is such a thing as *infernal* Grace, and it can galvanize, just for as long as may be necessary, that adorable shape which, according to St Catherine of Siena, stinks in all its parts.[2]

The citation itself, which is characteristic of Mauriac's taste,

1 *Desert*, p. 162f.
2 *Enemy*, p. 198.

gives the case away, even if we have not suspected before that the description is becoming homiletic. Or again here one sentence betrays the shift: Hervé is setting off to spend the evening with his mistress; the passage starts off in his own mind, with his thoughts about how to deceive his mother, and then we can see his mind being faded away and Mauriac's mind being slipped in instead:

> He [Hervé] promised to do his best and she [his mother] understood quite clearly that he would not return home before evening. He sat with his face turned away from her. Nothing could prevent him from doing this afternoon what he intended to do, from savouring to the full his sorry delight, from plunging into surroundings which could not even be imagined by this elderly woman in front of him.[1]

At least these intrusions are not as crude as the unblushing remark in *Le Démon de Connaissance*. Maryan, the hero, has been day-dreaming how to create his soul a model of Francis, Dominic, Ignatius; and the text continues: 'Ainsi délire cet orgueilleux: comme il est loin du Maître humble de coeur! Mais il ne le sait pas'.[2] But there is a parenthesis in a later and maturer novel which is almost as disconcerting. The priest, Alain Forcas, wakes one morning at a later hour than he had meant to:

> The Angelus. And he had meant to get up at dawn! It was already full day . . . He ran to the window and pushed open the shutters . . . He would leave off shaving till after Mass (though he was not one of those priests who have the effrontery to approach the altar uncleansed). He must hurry . . . . . [etc.][3]

Can we not, in that parenthesis, see M. Mauriac getting ready to write a letter of complaint to the bishop? Occasionally he reads a lesson from the Catechism to his characters—sometimes even literally:

> The child [Marie de Lados' little boy] sat with his elbows propped upon it [the table], busy with his Catechism . . .

1 *Lost*, p. 49.
2 *Récits*, p. 214. ('Thus did this swollen-head deliriously dream: what a long way he was from the humble-hearted Master! But he did not know it.')
3 *Angels*, p. 215f.

43

He was still muttering to himself: '*Are there then three Gods?*'—as though he did not know that there is but one— one sole and single Love.[1]

This time we can hear the Sunday-School master prodding the boy, and saying: 'Come now, you do know, don't you, that there is but one . . .?'

Even more abrupt is the spiritual counsel delivered to Brigitte Pian, ill-concealed beneath a negative. It starts from her own thoughts, and then the announcer's voice breaks in to the script:

> Was she a saint? She was making great efforts to be one, and, at each step forward, fought hard to hold the ground she had gained. No one had ever told her that the closer a man gets to sanctity the more conscious does he become of his own worthlessness, his own nothingness, and gives to God . . . all credit for the few good activities with which Grace has endowed him.[2]

But these blemishes are so obvious as to stare one in the face; and in most of these passages Mauriac has given us some slight warning that he is moving out of the congregation to preach a retreat from the pulpit. What is more disturbing, because less easily detectable, is the second type of intrusion, where he ventriloquizes from within the characters, so to speak. Let us start with an early example of what might be called the author's internal (as opposed to external) intrusion. Jérome and Vincent, the young Catholic Social leaders, are discussing whether to exploit the enthusiasm of Jean-Paul (the hero of the novel):

> 'We'll have to be careful', said Vincent: 'Jean-Paul will resist: he's got some character.'
> The Leader seemed anxious. 'So much the worse', said he [sc. Jérome]: 'I want to have round me people with docile temperaments, not personalities who stand up to me'.[3]

What has happened here? Clearly Mauriac has mentally composed this about Jérome in the third person ('he is the sort

---

[1] *Genetrix*, p. 180.
[2] *Pharisees*, p. 133.
[3] *L'Enfant*, p. 61. ('Je veux autour de moi des tempéraments qui me servent, non des personnalités qui me résistent.')

who wants to have round him people with docile temper-
aments . . .', etc.) and has then carelessly written it direct into
the first person. The result is unconvincing—for who in fact
would say this of himself, even to one of his own henchmen?
And this defect is not confined to the early novels; two examples
must suffice, both from one of his most successful. Both occur
in the diary of the protagonist, Louis. The first, addressed to his
wife Isa, reminds her of their time of courting. She had always
said to Louis:

'I fell in love with you from the moment we met. We had
said many, many prayers at Lourdes . . . and as soon as I set
my eye on you, I knew that they had been answered.'
You were far from guessing [Louis comments] how those
words grated on my nerves. Those who oppose you in religion
have, really, a very much nobler idea of it than you realize,
or than they realize themselves . . .[1]

Those last words, italicised, give the case away: the old man has
ceased to speak, or rather to write in his diary, and Mauriac
is whispering behind him. Much later in the novel the old
grandfather Louis again is talking to Janine, whom he has taken
in after the collapse of her marriage with Phili. He, the pro-
fessed agnostic, suddenly mentions her faith: surely, he asks,
that will help her in her trouble? Janine is puzzled by this, and
finally rejects the suggestion. She says that

she didn't like mixing up religion with matters of this kind,
that she was a practising Christian and regularly performed
her religious duties, but that she had a horror of morbidity.
She might have been saying that she always paid her taxes.
It is precisely the attitude that, all my life, I have loathed and
detested, the caricature and mean interpretation of the
Christian life which I had deliberately chosen to regard as
the essence of the religious mind, in order that I might feel
free to hate it.[2]

It is true that here the translator has made Mauriac sound
rather cruder than he is. The sentence 'I had deliberately
chosen to regard . . .' actually runs in the original 'j'avais feint
d'y voir . . .', which is much less objectionable. Yet even with

[1] *Knot*, p. 48 (italics mine).
[2] Ibid., p. 198.

that slight qualification, do we not feel a subtle slide of the ground towards the end of the paragraph? Even granted the awkward technique, the confession-journal, which Mauriac has elected to employ in this novel, can we really believe that it is still Louis speaking, writing himself: 'I pretended to consider this the acme of religious thought so that I could hate it with justification'? Or do we not rather sense at this point that it is again Mauriac who has stepped in to dot the i's and cross the t's of self-analysis? 'Pour avoir le droit de la haïr'—is that what a man, even a Louis, writes of himself? I shall not go so far as to say with M. Sartre that this is not novel-writing; but there is something seriously wrong with a work that pulls us up to ask these questions.

(iv) There is a second kind of disquiet which we feel also when Mauriac intrudes, especially when he intrudes with a *Gratia ex machina,* and the source of this disquiet is worth examining. Let us take some examples. When old Félicité Cazenave is dying, her only consolation is the sight of her son Fernand when he comes to visit her in the evenings:

> For her the whole long day was but preliminary to these evening hours. Her eyes were taking their last fill of him before darkness should overwhelm them . . .
> Only when it was hard upon the third hour was the sponge offered to the victim. How much more bitter than gall was the sight, upon that taut and suffering face, of so much love offered to another! Yet Félicité Cazenave felt dimly that it was a good thing she should suffer for her son. What she did not know was that she had been crucified.[1]

This rather nauseating importation of echoes from Good Friday is not only in bad taste, but is quite gratuitous. But something like it, though less crude, occurs in a much maturer novel, *That Which was Lost.* When Alain is beginning to shake himself free from Tota, he begins also to have a premonition of his future priestly vocation.

> In future . . . many others would clutch on to him and he would have to bear the weight not of one but of many . . .
> A vocation. It is not for nothing that a man is set apart

1 *Genetrix*, p. 187.

from his fellows and marked, even before he reaches manhood. Alain had in good faith been retracing the delectable reaches of his life back through the years and now here was the wellspring at last; a little hill, crowned with a malefactor's cross glimpsed through the everlasting clouds of contumely, hatred and love that cling to it, and surrounded by the terrifying indifference of the world (the ancient and oft repeated act, the heedless arm thrusting the same lance home).[1]

When we find these sudden invocations of the act of Redemption why is it that we feel embarrassed? Why, again, do we feel restive when we read this, for instance, of the death of Irène:

Sinking, drowning, she could not regain the surface and the air; her strength was gone. She clutched frenziedly, until her nails were broken, her elbows torn and bleeding. The great discovery was not for her; not hers to fall upon her knees, to weep for joy . . . She must pass through this darkness into which she had so madly plunged now to the bitter end. But as she slipped into the very abyss she knew, she saw, she cried aloud at last unto that love by the name which is above all other names.[2]

The restiveness which this induces in us is by no means allayed when we learn that the unknown priest who hears Mme de Blénauge's confession has the sudden intuition that Irène died in the presence of Christ.[3] For though the scene is beautifully portrayed, it strikes us as having something arbitrary, something willed *ab extra*, at its core. The same is even true of the much more modest, more tentative ending of *Galigaï* to which Mauriac, as we have seen above,[4] himself refers. Nicolas Plassac walks away from his home, his love having foundered.

He walked alone, a prey to this sad hunger which all the kingdoms of the earth could not have appeased, alone with this tenderness, which had withdrawn from all human faces and remained spread out like the sea under the mindless stars. At the place where a clearing among the trees revealed a wide patch of sky, he stopped, turned his head, and saw,

1 *Lost*, p. 143f.
2 Ibid., p. 98.
3 Ibid., p. 110.
4 Vide. sup., p. 37.

47

all mixed up with the roof-tops, the black abandoned cathedral. Yet the human termites had built this enormous nave to the measure of the love which smothers some of them. Nicolas Plassac walked on to the spot where the road crosses the Leyrot. A stranger to himself, detached from all creatures, he sat on the parapet, and he stayed there as if he had arranged to meet someone.[1]

It is effective in its way; yet even here there is a moment's disquiet as we read it, which can be defined perhaps by the sudden and uncalled-for occurrence of the words 'les insectes humains'. Can it be that the sense of artificiality, of the *voulu*, which we feel in all these however distant invocations of Rescue, lies in this: that the pictures of the Wreck itself, which the rescue-squad is called in to deal with, are artificial and in the last resort arbitrary?

This requires further clarification. No one should object to Mauriac for his realistic desire to depict a fallen world. Those who do so object, have surely allowed their dislike of theology to cloud the clarity of their vision. And more, from a picture of the Fall a genuine and valid apologetic for the Faith can be constructed. But it must in that case be a *genuine* picture of the Fall. And a genuine picture of the Fall requires two conditions: a realisation, first, of the primal innocence; and, second, a real compassion for the fallen *qua* fallen. It is precisely these two requirements, I think, that we find so often missing in Mauriac's work. Whenever Mauriac discusses Port-Royal or Pascal, as he does in many of his works, he almost tumbles over backwards in his eagerness to dissociate himself from the Jansenist heresy. But the influence always remained. In an address, already cited, to the students of his old college, Grand-Lebrun, in 1951, he paid tribute to his old teacher who, among other things, taught him to love Pascal and Racine:

> You didn't only introduce them into my memory as an examinee, but into the most secret places of my mind and flesh—which perhaps you have had to expiate by an extra spell of Purgatory, for it is you indeed who in no small part have made me the novelist I have become.[2]

But it is the two requirements above-mentioned whose absence

[1] *Galigaï*, p. 168.
[2] *La Table Ronde*, l.c., p. 43.

marks the Jansenist: and we cannot but feel that Mauriac never really got Port-Royal out of his system.[1]

This is most clearly seen in some of his pictures of sexual relations. It is true that Mauriac tries to dissociate himself from the view of old Mme Dézaymeries. She wrote to her Director:

> I remember reading in Pascal that marriage is the lowest of all Christian states, vile and unpleasing to God. How strongly I feel the truth of that! How convinced I am that the traffic of the flesh is a grim and filthy business.[2]

And the priest has to reply that it is 'very reprehensible on her part to espouse the derogatory views of a heretic on that great Sacrament'. But consider the searing pictures the author gives us, and even sometimes seems to delight in giving us, of the sexual relations between, e.g., Noémie and Jean Péloueyre:

> Long was the battle waged by Jean Péloueyre, at first with his own ice-bound senses, and then with the woman who was as one dead. As day was dawning a stifled groan marked the end of a struggle that had lasted six long hours. Soaked with sweat, Jean Péloueyre dared not make a movement. He lay there, looking more hideous than a worm beside the corpse it has at last abandoned.[3]

or between Thérèse and Bernard Desqueyroux:

> Nothing is so severing as the frenzy that seizes upon our partner in the act. I always saw Bernard as a man who charged head-down at pleasure, while I lay like a corpse, motionless, as though fearing that, at the slightest gesture on my part, this madman, this epileptic, might strangle me. As often as not, balanced on the very edge of ultimate excruciation, he would discover suddenly that he was alone. The gloomy battle would be broken off, and Bernard, retracing his steps, would, as it were, stand back and see me there, like a dead body thrown up on the shore, my teeth clenched, my body cold to the touch.[4]

[1] Cf. the passage cited above, implying a rigorous form of predestination, p. 41, sup.
[2] *Enemy*, p. 194.
[3] *Leper*, p. 43.
[4] *Thérèse*, p. 30 (and cf. p. 38).

These pictures, though they have an appearance of justification in their contexts, are given with a little too much relish; and they do not encourage us to think that Mauriac's dissociation from Mme Dézaymeries's view is so radical after all. Young Louis in the *Woman of the Pharisees* comes to conclusions which he may, of course, owe to some extent to his step-mother Brigitte, but which Mauriac at least does not do anything ostensibly to correct:

> My views on this matter have not greatly changed. I believe that all the miseries of our human state come from our inability to remain chaste, and that men vowed to chastity would be spared most of the evils that weigh them down . . . Wherever I have found it [happiness based on generosity and love], the movements of the heart and the promptings of the flesh have been kept under strict discipline.[1]

No doubt this is meant to convey the thoughts of a priggish young man—though we must remember that he is supposed to be writing years after the event. But we cannot feel that Mauriac is so far away. And this is perhaps confirmed by a much more casual, and therefore a more revealing, remark the author throws out in another novel. Fabien is returning to Paris after the Easter holidays.

> The old stones of palaces and bridges lay basking in the soft radiance of a misty sun. The city was full of young bodies responsive to the call of spring, meeting at every corner, sitting on the terrace of every café. The air was full of stale romance. It was the time of year when *the enemy within us* finds a ready ally in the outward scene . . . A thousand posters called temptingly from the sun-baked walls. It was that season when the streets are full of faces that no longer try to hide their secret yearning, when parted lips and seeking eyes take no account of the dangerous abyss.[2]

We have no wish to deny that there is an 'enemy within'; but that he should so immediately spring to mind at the mention of spring is surely suggestive of Mauriac's preoccupations.

It is, indeed, the casual phrase, the imagery that comes spontaneously to the pen, that best reveals an author's deepest

[1] *Pharisees*, p. 119.
[2] *Enemy*, p. 181 (italics mine).

convictions. And here we have plenty of evidence to hand. Jérome, the writer in *Un Homme de Lettres*, exclaims:

> Besides, happy love, now: does it exist? Oh yes, it does! It exists in a land we do not know. I believe in the existence of satisfied lovers in the same way that I believe in the existence of angels. Somewhere or other there is harp-music, the beating of wings—But where?[1]

Hardly once in the novels do we come across a happy marriage —except the vaguely delineated but moving relationship between old Brigitte Pian and the doctor, and one delicate and just passage on fidelity, which, however, does not occur in a novel but in the *Journal*.

> How few love-affairs find enough strength within themselves to remain sedentary! Perhaps that is why married love which persists through countless vicissitudes seems to me the loveliest of miracles, though it is the commonest. After many years, still to have so many things to say to each other, from the most trivial to the most serious, without the intention or the desire to astonish or to be admired—what a wonderful thing! No need to tell lies to each other: lying is no use from now on, husband and wife have become so transparent to each other. That is the only love which loves immobility, which feeds on habit and the daily event.[2]

But do we ever in the novels see a hint of this? The normal attitude there is this, from the introduction to *Trois Récits*: 'How can lovers escape their métier of executioner? They are not gods: they are not God'.[3] Or this, describing Paula's loathing for her mother-in-law, the Baronne de Galéas: 'We speak of "making love": we should be able, too, to speak of "making hate". To make hate is comforting. It rests the mind and relaxes the nerves'.[4] Or, for the imagery that accompanies this frame of mind, there is this, when Alain Forcas comes across Thérèse in the park: 'There on an iron chair, with her back against the shaft of a lamp, was a woman seated upright with her head thrown back as if in the act of offering her throat to

1 *Récits*, p. 97.
2 *Journal*, p. 38.
3 *Récits*, p. xix.
4 *Misery*, p. 42.

51

the knife'.[1] Or, more cruelly, this picture of the old Baronne:

> Hatred had quickened the senile jerking of the aged head which was bare and bald and prepared already for the nothingness of death ... The Baronne kept turning and twisting her bald vulture's head among the pillows.[2]

What in fact we feel from all this kind of imagery is not so much that Mauriac is mistaken in thinking of the world as fallen and needing Grace—the Christian believes this, and the non-Christian frequently agrees: but rather that what Mauriac is picturing as fallen is in fact only diseased. Because he has a clinical, almost a purely physiological, conception of the fallen state, so he naturally tends to have a chemist's conception of redemption. Grace is injected or swallowed whole like a pill. It is simply the first conception that is wrong. Mauriac's sinners are frequently not sinners at all, or not sinners in the particular aspects that he underlines, but unreal creatures seen through a sombre lens. And at his best moments Mauriac himself is aware of this. It is with a remarkably lucid self-knowledge that he said once of his own writing:

> I had hoped that Mozart, who had opened me the gates of his paradise, would suddenly release a flight of angels in my work—angels who would not be 'dark angels'. But as soon as I set to work, everything takes on a colour according to my eternal colours; even my most beautiful characters enter into a kind of sulphurous light which is natural to me and which I do not defend—for it is simply mine.[3]

IV

Achievement

The divergent estimates of Mauriac's place as a novelist are most striking. We have had M. Sartre's severe judgement that he is not a novelist at all. Elsewhere, on the other hand, he has been described variously as: 'unrivalled by any living

---

[1] *Lost,* p. 59f.

[2] *Misery,* pp. 101, 109 ('the nothingness of death' translates 'le néant'; and 'her bald .. etc.' translates 'sa vieille tête de rapace').

[3] *Journal,* p. 220.

novelist in any country' (Mr Raymond Mortimer): 'perhaps the greatest living European novelist' (Mr A. Calder-Marshall): and so on. Mr Graham Greene[1] and M. Mauriac himself[2] have exchanged mutual eulogies. But Miss Helen Gardner[3] has tried to define Mauriac's success precisely by a contrast with Mr Graham Greene and the English Catholic novels:

> They [the latter] are constructions which can be used to express their author's views on good and evil, the natural and the supernatural; [whereas] the solid bourgeois and peasant world of M. Mauriac has an existence of its own apart from its author's beliefs.

Moreover, the confidence of the English writers about the destiny of their characters compares unfavourably, she says,

> with M. Mauriac's reticence and religious agnosticism about the ultimate fate of his main characters. Though no living writer excels him in suggesting, in some of his minor figures, the grace of holiness, he shows towards the creatures of his imagination the humility and respect that is owing to persons.

We can only sigh, *Utinam semper sit!* Miss Gardner is a fine critic; but the evidence presented in the previous chapter must surely qualify so totally favourable a judgement. What, on balance, are we then to conclude?

(i) Mauriac's most widely acknowledged achievement consists in his style. And we do not mean by that, of course, that he merely has certain purple passages to his credit, but that his writing does normally do its work so well. It may be an exaggeration to say, as M. Gaéton Bernoville does, that he is, 'along with Montherlant, the greatest living prose-writer in the French language'[4], but the distinction of his style cannot be denied. Even in novels that as a whole are failures we find the characteristic and effective Mauriac periods occurring. Denis

1 Essay 'François Mauriac' in *The Lost Childhood*, 1951.
2 Essay 'Graham Greene' in *Great Men*.
3 Article 'François Mauriac: A Woman of the Pharisees', in *Penguin New Writing*, No. 31, 1947.
4 'Réflections sur l'état présent de la Littérature Catholique', as Pref. to R. North, p. xxxii. The best study of Mauriac's style occurs in the chapter 'l'Expression' in Mlle Nelly Cormeau's otherwise over-enthusiastic book (Cormeau, Chap. VI).

Revolou, for instance, has been talking to his sister Rose in the paddock; she leaves him, and the sounds of hidden life, disturbed by their conversation, now begin again:

> Sounds of summer evenings that rise in us from the depths of our unhappy childhood. He seemed in his misery to have taken root. For the insects he might have been a tree. A butterfly, of the kind known as 'aiguillons', perched on his shoulders, opening and shutting its wings. Ants clung to this strange trunk of woven stuff. Beetles and cockchafers boomed in the lower leaves of the oaks which the sun had turned to flame. This was how one ought to die—growing into death by sheer virtue of immobility, feeling the blood turn to sap, slipping without effort into the vegetable world, passing from one place to another, from love and wretchedness to sleep, which is but another form of life.[1]

Or, if we want something more directly human, here are Raymond Courrèges's memories of the early-morning tram journeys on which he first got to know Maria Cross:

> Nothing in his life had ever meant so much to him as those moments when they had sat facing one another in a crowd of poor work-people with coal-blackened faces and heads drooping with sleep. He could see the scene in imagination— a newspaper slipping to the floor from a hand gone numb; a bare-headed woman holding up her novelette to catch the light of the lamps, her lips moving as though in prayer. He could hear again the great raindrops splashing in the dust of the lane behind the church at Talence, could watch the passing figure of a workman crouched over the handlebar of his bicycle, a canvas sack, with a bottle protruding from it, slung over his shoulder. The trees behind the railings were stretching out their dusty leaves like hands begging for water.[2]

In the original the slightly pathetic, and perhaps also patronising, tone that attends the words 'poor work-people . . .', etc, is less marked. The picture is hazy, perhaps; but that is what a reminiscence should be, and within its limits it is very successful.

[1] *Sea*, p. 107.
[2] *Desert*, p. 147f.

What Mauriac so powerfully conveys in both these passages is the sense of and the significance of a situation—the place, the people, the particularity of the moment. One last example must suffice; and this time, since to discuss style without reference to the original is absurd, I shall quote both the French and the English. Louis is describing in his diary how, after his wife Isa's death, he goes back to visit Calèse.

Les ormes des routes et les peupliers des prairies dessinent de larges plans superposés, et entre leur lignes sombres la brume s'accumule,—la brume et la fumée des feux d'herbes, et cette haleine immense de la terre qui a bu. Car nous nous réveillons en plein automne et les grappes, où un peu de pluie demeure prise et brille, ne retrouveront plus ce dont les a frustrées l'août pluvieux. Mais pour nous, peut-être n'est il jamais trop tard. J'ai besoin de me répéter qu'il n'est jamais trop tard.
[He goes into his wife's old room].
Le désœuvrement, cette disponibilité totale dont je ne sais si je jouis ou si je souffre à la campagne, cela seul m'incita à pousser la porte entrebaîllée . . . Les domestiques avaient fait place nette, et le soleil dévorait, jusque dans les moindres encoignures, les restes impalpables d'une destinée finie. L'après-midi de septembre bourdonnait de mouches réveillées. Les tilleuls épais et ronds ressemblaient à des fruits touchés. L'azur, foncé au zenith, palissait contre les collines endormies. Un éclat de rire jaillisait d'une fille que je ne voyais pas; des chapeaux de soleil bougeaient au ras des vignes: les vendanges étaient commencées.
Mais la vie merveilleuse s'était retirée de la chambre d'Isa; et au bas de l'armoire, une paire de gants, une ombrelle avaient l'air mort . . .[1]

1 *Le Noeud de Vipères*, pp. 126-8, *Knot*, pp. 178-9: 'The elms along the roads and the poplars in the meadows stand massed together. Between their dark-hued trunks the mist accumulates, and the smoke of bonfires, and the breath of the huge earth when it has drunk deep. For we have waked to find the autumn all about us. The grapes still glittering from the recent storm will never recover what this rainy August stole. But for us, perhaps, it is never too late. I must never stop telling myself that it is never too late.
What led me there was idleness, that complete lack of occupation which seizes me in the country. I never know whether I most enjoy or dislike it. I was tempted to push the half-open door . . . The servants had swept the place clean, and the sun, even in the farthest corners, had eaten up the last impalpable remains of a completed destiny. The September afternoon was buzzing with sleepy flies. The thick round tops of the lime trees looked like bruised fruit. The blue, deep at the zenith, showed

It is extremely effective, because simple and economical. The rhythm is sometimes a little too close to poetry ('et cette haleine immense de la terre qui a bu') but it carries us on without drawing attention to itself. And the situation is vividly conveyed by the natural and unforced contrasts: the contrast between the heavy weight of the rain upon the vine crop and the hope that man must cling to, and the opposite contrast that follows between the vigour and joy of harvesting and the dead room from which 'la vie merveilleuse s'était retirée' and which is marked now only by the flotsam of life—gloves and an umbrella. There are not many writers left who can so convey 'the spirit of place'.

(ii) Moreover, since Mauriac is usually thought of as the author of long, weighted and atmospheric periods, it is worth remembering that he also can achieve the pregnant phrase. For a writer who as a whole is so humourless, the occasional flashes of epigrammatic wit are striking. On All Souls' Eve 1939 he suddenly observes in his diary: 'This night of November 1st the dead from the Great War have grown twenty years younger'.[1] Old Louis takes the hand of Marinette 'as I might have taken the hand of an unhappy child, and like a child she leaned her head upon my shoulder. I received the gift of it merely because I happened to be there. The earth receives the fallen peach'.[2] Brigitte Pian 'buried her grievances and dug them up weeks later when no one remembered what had caused them.'[3] Gilles in the middle of a conversation with Mme Agathe suddenly forgets her and thinks only of his friend Nicolas, whom she wants to marry, but whom Gilles will not release: 'He forgot this woman in the corner of the room, a bat clinging to the curtains'.[4] A friend is 'someone who helps you to throw a corpse into the water without asking any questions'.[5] (How characteristic of Mauriac, this metaphor!) And, a last example, Gabriel Gradère has been arguing with Mathilde Desbats about her plan to marry her daughter, Catharine, to Andrès. She

pale behind the dozing hills. A burst of laughter came up to me from some girl I could not see. Sun-bonnets were moving among the vines. The grape-harvest had begun.

But the wonder of life had withdrawn from Isa's room. A pair of gloves and an umbrella lying on the floor of the wardrobe looked dead . . .'

[1] *Journal*, p. 420.
[2] *Knot*, p. 93. (The original is even more concise: 'je la reçevais parce que j'étais là; l'argile reçoit une pêche qui se détache,' p. 108.)
[3] *Pharisees*, p. 67.
[4] *Galigaï*, p. 57.
[5] Ibid., p. 68.

considers it only a *mariage de convenance*, but Gabriel insists on what it involves: 'Nothing will be changed', she says; but Gabriel points out that they'll be sleeping in the same room—indeed, in the same bed. 'All right, then—in the same bed', she exclaims, pretending to laugh it off. But 'Gabriel detected a note of suffering in her voice. It was as though he were holding a pigeon in his hands and pressing it rather too tightly'.[1]

(iii) This last is also a good instance of the way in which Mauriac handles the relationships *between* his characters. Indeed, these relationships are usually more delicately presented than the characters seen full-face—which reveals the direct relationship between them and the author. Put in another way, Mauriac's characters are better commentators on each other than he is on them. There is, for instance, a beautiful tact in the relationship between old Dr Courrèges and his beloved Maria Cross, especially in the well-known scene where he gives her a medical examination.[2] Earlier in the same novel there is a dramatic scene when Mme Courrèges declares that the death of Maria Cross's illegitimate boy is God's judgement, and the doctor stamps out of the room.[3] Some of the overheard conversations of the rapacious and plotting sons and daughters-in-law, recorded by the old man Louis in *The Knot of Vipers* are effective;[4] and so too is the embarrassed conversation between him and his natural son Robert, the ne'er-do-well.[5] The growing understanding between the wild, suspicious, ungovernable Jean Mirbel and the Abbé Calou[6] could hardly be bettered. The scene, too, when Brigitte travels to Octave's death-bed—the first time that cracks begin to show in her marmoreal self-conceit—the train journey, with Brigitte's step-children silent, and she imploring, and shrinking in size as they look at her: this is superb.[7] And finally there is the close of the same novel, too hurried and sketchy perhaps, as we have admitted above,[8] but wonderfully restrained, and without any forced attempt to make out Brigitte as a saint.

Even in the novel which M. Sartre has criticized so severely,

1 *Angels*, p. 207.
2 *Desert*, p. 129f.
3 Ibid., p. 17.
4 *Knot*, e.g., pp. 122-5.
5 Ibid., pp. 142-4.
6 *Pharisees*, e.g. pp. 107-9.
7 Ibid., p. 171.
8 Vide sup., p. 32.

The End of the Night, we must acknowledge the gentleness with which Thérèse treats her daughter and shakes off the would-be lover, George—the gentleness with which, in fact, she expiates her crime. And in one of Mauriac's most successful novels, *The Knot of Vipers*, it is remarkable how the characters, especially the wife, Isa, gradually emerge in their true light through and in spite of the distorting narration by Louis, the protagonist. Even the oppressive *Genetrix* succeeds brilliantly in suggesting first the tyranny of the mother over the son, and then the 'counter-attack' by the dead wife from beyond the grave. The psychological understanding in these cases, and many others, is acquired by letting the characters *be*, without *arrières-pensées* about their eternal destiny. The paradox is that it is precisely then that their salvation or damnation becomes most significant and most believable. Mauriac has the misfortune (in one sense) to be a believing writer in an unbelieving age. A novelist like Manzoni can move freely, largely, within his total Catholic world. Mauriac has the advantage which the Faith gives him of realism, honesty and spiritual penetration. But he cannot all the time exclude from his attention the heretic, the sceptic or the atheist who exist in the same world; they peep over the window-sill as he writes, and whenever he lets their presence distract him, his writing falters. When, as in the above instances, he gives his characters freedom to be the persons they are, they then become truly damnable or redeemable— and this is the real, the only real, task of the Catholic novelist in this or any age.

(iv) All this must be set on the credit side of what we have presented so far as a heavily debit account. And, to show that it is not a question of singling out chance passages and accidental successes for commendation, but of a genuine, if seriously qualified, achievement, let us end with some reference to the (in my view) most totally successful of the novels: *Le Mystère Frontenac*.[1] What probably gives it its consistency is that the thread running through it—family loyalty and the grip of 'place'—is nearest to Mauriac's own heart:

---

[1] As critics have been divided about the merits of Mauriac himself, so too they have been divided about the relative merits of the novels. Emile Rideau considers *Knot* the *chef d'oeuvre* of Catholic novels (Rideau, p. 67). Nelly Cormeau, surprisingly, singles out the short story, *Coups de Couteau*, as the summit of his art (Cormeau, p. 119). I think it sufficient to say that the novels which will endure are *Frontenac*, *Knot*, *Pharisees*, *Angels*, *Thérèse*, *Night*, and perhaps *Destins*.

'They leave nothing to chance' [cries Yves Frontenac], 'they organize everybody's happiness; they don't understand that we want to be happy in a different way.'

'It isn't a question, for them, of happiness' [replies Jean-Louis, his brother], 'but of acting for the common good and in the interest of the family. No, it isn't a question of happiness. Have you noticed? It's a word that never appears on their lips—happiness.'[1]

Sheltered and linked together by the family—Blanche, the mother, and the gruff, affectionate Uncle Xavier,—the children prolong their infancy as long as possible. But Yves is set apart, the boy poet, the quiet one who ponders the mystery of suffering as he watches an ant struggling in the sand.[2] He resists the divine vocation that comes to him, dismissing it as his own voice. For a time he runs wild in Paris, but the call comes again when he is at the end of his tether. In the thick of the traffic and bustling humanity of Paris he suddenly sees his old home, the Landes:

> Around him human beings and cars twisted, mingled, separated at the cross-roads, and he felt himself as solitary as long ago, in the middle of the narrow space where, surrounded with ferns and bushes, he used to lie hid, a little boy run wild. The uniform din of the road was like the soft noises of nature, and the passers-by were more strangers to him than the pines of Bourideys whose tops once watched over this little Frontenac nestling at their feet in the thickest part of the undergrowth. To-day these men and women buzzed like the flies in the Landes, hesitated like dragon-flies, and one of them sometimes landed down beside Yves, against his sleeve, without even seeing him, and then flew off. But how muffled and distant the voice had become which pursued the Frontenac child, at the bottom of his lair, and which he sensed again at this moment.[3]

This use of the 'flash-back' is a familiar technique, but it is just right in its place. The death of old Uncle Xavier, who pathetically had wanted till the last to conceal from the children the fact (which they knew all along) that he had a mistress,

1 *Frontenac*, p. 122.
2 Ibid., p. 140ff.
3 Ibid., pp. 272-4.

is an emotional turning-point both in the novel and in Yves's experience; and the elderly mistress herself, Joséfa, common and unattractive, small-minded but intensely loyal, is presented (for once in Mauriac's novels) with real compassion. In the end Yves is reconciled to family and place through a severe illness, during which his elder brother visits him; the superbly quiet, tactful visit of the dull, prosy, affectionate Jean-Louis is beautifully handled.

It will be seen that the range of this novel is limited. There are none of the violent passions, the tremendous collapses and sudden deliverances, that some of Mauriac's other novels attempt—and so rarely achieve. But perhaps for that very reason it is on the whole consistently effective. The bitterness has been absorbed into the moss, the marsh, the resin of the Landes; and here at last in one of his novels we find what Mauriac says that the poets give him.

All of them, whether they believed in eternal life, or like Anna de Noailles denied it, bear witness to the grandeur of the human soul, its divine vocation. The poets have always protected me against doubt. Even though they may be covered in mud, like Rimbaud and Verlaine, they awaken in us the sentiment of a paradisal purity, of a lost purity which we must recover in self-abasement and in tears.[1]

[1] *Journal*, p. 63f.

SELECT BIBLIOGRAPHY

The following are listed in order of publication; titles of English translations (where available) are followed, in square brackets, by the abbreviated titles used in the foot-notes.

NOVELS

L'Enfant Chargé de Chaînes, 1913 [*L'Enfant*].
La Robe Prétexte, 1914 [*Robe*].
La Chair et le Sang, 1920 [*Chair*].
Préséances, 1921.
Le Baiser au Lépreux (*A Kiss for the Leper*), 1922 [*Leper*].
Genitrix (*Genetrix*), 1923 [*Genetrix*].
Le Fleuve de Feu, 1923 [*Fleuve*].
Le Mal (*The Enemy*), 1924 [*Enemy*].
Le Désert de l'Amour (*The Desert of Love*), 1925 [*Desert*].
Coups de Couteau, 1926 [*Coups*].
Un Homme de Lettres, 1926 [*Lettres*].
Thérèse Desqueyroux (*Thérèse*), 1927 [*Therese*].
Le Démon de Connaissance, 1928 [*Démon*].
Destins, 1928.
Ce Qui était Perdu (*That Which was Lost*), 1930 [*Lost*].
Le Noeud de Vipères (*The Knot of Vipers*), 1932 [*Knot*].
Le Mystère Frontenac (*The Frontenac Mystery*), 1933 [*Frontenac*].
La Fin de la Nuit (*The End of the Night*), 1935 [*Night*].
Les Anges Noirs (*The Dark Angels*), 1936 [*Angels*].
Plongées (*Studies*), 1938.
Les Chemins de la Mer (*The Unknown Sea*), 1939 [*Sea*].
La Pharisienne (*Woman of the Pharisees*), 1941 [*Pharisees*].
Le Sagouin (*The Little Misery*), 1951 [*Misery*].
Galigaï, (*The Loved and the Unloved*) 1952 [*Galigaï*].

PLAYS

Asmodée (*Asmodée, or The Intruder*), 1938 [*Asmodée*].
Les Mal-Aimés, 1945 [*Aimés*].
Le Passage du Malin, 1948 [*Malin*].

GENERAL

Commencements d'une Vie, 1932 [*Commencements*].
Dieu et Mammon (*God and Mammon*), 1929 [*Mammon*].
Mes Grands Hommes (*Great Men*), 1950 [*Great Men*].
La Pierre d'Achoppement, 1951 [*Pierre*].

STUDIES

Charles du Bos: *François Mauriac et le problème du romancier catholique*, 1933 [du Bos].
Georges Hourdin: *Mauriac, Romancier Chrétien*, 1945 [Hourdin].
Joseph Majault: *Mauriac et l'art du roman*, 1946 [Majault].
Emile Rideau: *François Mauriac*, 1947 [Rideau].
Nelly Cormeau: *L'Art de François Mauriac*, 1951 [Cormeau].
Robert J. North: *Le Catholicisme dans l'oeuvre de François Mauriac*, 1950 [North].